Handy New Mexico Genealogy Handbook

I0412039

Gary L. Morris

ISBN-13: 978-1508432142

ISBN-10: 1508432147

Table of Contents

Introduction   4
Brief History of New Mexico   5,6
Important Dates in New Mexico   7
Famous Battles Fought in New Mexico   8
Research Tips   9
Archives and Libraries   10,11
Genealogical and Historical Societies   12
Mailing Lists and Message Boards   13
Newspapers and Periodicals   14,15
Maps and Gazetteers   16
City Directories   17
Vital Records   18,19
Census Records   20,21
Church Records   22-24
Military Records   2527
Cemetery Records and Obituaries   28,29
Wills and Probate Records   30
Immigration and Naturalization Records   31
Native American Records   32
Missing Matriarchs (Women's Resources)   33
Common Surnames   34,35

Notes

Genealogical Research in New Mexico

Even though it is one of the youngest American states, there are many genealogical records and resources available for tracing your family history in New Mexico. Because there are so many records held at many different locations, tracking down the records for your ancestor can be an ominous task. Don't worry though, we know just where they are, and we'll show you which records you'll need, while helping you to understand:

1. What they are
2. Where to find them
3. How to use them

These records can be found both online and off, so we'll introduce you to online websites, indexes and databases, as well as brick-and-mortar repositories and other institutions that will help with your research in New Mexico. So that you will have a more comprehensive understanding of these records, we have provided a brief history of the "Land of Enchantment" to illustrate what type of records may have been generated during specific time periods. That information will assist you in pinpointing times and locations on which to focus the search for your New Mexico ancestors and their records.

A Brief History of New Mexico

There is evidence that humans have occupied the area that is now New Mexico from around 20,000 years ago. Since then it has been home to the semi-nomadic Basket Makers, the Cochise, the Cliff Dwellers, or Anasazi, who were predecessors of the modern Pueblo Indians. The Navajo also settled in new Mexico, as did the Apache, who became a threat to any white settlers entering the region.

Francisco Vásquez de Coronado led the first expedition to New Mexico, starting in 1540, and in 1598, Don Juan de Onate led an expedition to explore the Rio Grande. One year later Onate established the settlement of San Gabriel, in the vicinity of present-day Espanola. In 1610 the Spanish moved their center of activity to Santa Fe, and subsequently dominated the area for the next two centuries.

After gaining its independence from Spain in 1821, Mexico secured the region, which remained under their control for the next twenty five years. The Spanish settlers in the area resented the control of the Mexican officials and their inability to control the war-like Apaches. The unrest led to a bloody revolt in 1837 which was put down by forces led by General Manuel Armijo. General Armijo served as governor until American forces under the command of General Stephen Watts Kearny took the region without resistance in 1846.

Without authorization from the United States Congress, Kearny immediately attempted to make the region a U.S. Territory. After appointing the Indian trader Charles Bent as his civil governor, Kearny led his army towards California. While Kearny was gone, Bent was killed in an Indian and Mexican revolt which was quickly put down by another contingent of American forces. That action secured control of the area for the United States, though the area was not officially recognized as part of America until 1848 when the Mexican-American War ended.

The Compromise of 1850 made New Mexico a United States Territory, though its new status did not bring any immediate change to the area. An increasing number of people passing through the area via the Santa Fe Trail became interested in settling the area however, and before long clashes over land between the new arrivals and the original Spanish-speaking inhabitants. Violent confrontations flared up occasionally, though most of the fighting took place in the courts. This enabled suck lawyers as Thomas Benton Catron to amass large amounts of personal wealth, as native grantees were forced to pay for his services with land.

Between 1891 and 1904, 33 million acres of disputed land was processed by the federal courts. Land disputes were not the sole cause of violence during this time though, as the Civil war found its way into the new territory. In 1862, an army of Texans led by Confederate General Henry Hopkins Sibley, marched up the Rio Grande, and occupied Santa Fe. A hastily assembled troop of volunteers defeated Sibley and his forces at Glorieta Pass however, in a conflict that is often called the Gettysburg of the West.

Sixteen years later in 1878 a range war that lasted until1881 erupted between cattle ranchers and merchants. It was during this conflict that New Mexico's most infamous son, William H. Bonney, better known as Billy the Kid, began to shape the territory's image of a lawless region not fit for statehood. In spite of the tumult, New Mexico began to prosper, and when the Atchison, Topeka, & Santa Fe Railroad entered the territory in 1879, the economy accelerated further.

With the Indian threat resolved by the end of the 19th century, New Mexico pushed for statehood, which was granted in 1912 by Theodore Roosevelt, who had rode with many New Mexicans in the Rough Riders during the Spanish-American War.

Important Dates in New Mexico History

1598 – Spanish settlement at Santa Fe

1610 – Santa Fe made provincial capitol

1680 – Pueblo Indian revolt drives white settlers from the area

1693 – Settlers return to Santa Fe

1706 – Albuquerque founded

1821 – Becomes province of Mexico

1846 – US forces occupy Santa Fe

1848 – Ceded to the United States in treaty of Guadalupe-Hidalgo

1850 – Organized as US Territory

1868 – Navajo reservations established

1870 – Apache reservations established

1912 - Statehood

Famous Battles Fought in New Mexico

The major battles that took place in New Mexico occurred during the Mexican American War and the US Civil War. The **Battle of El Brazito**, the first real battle in the Mexican-American War, and the **Siege of Pueblo de Taos** which ended it were also the bloodiest battles of the war.

The first skirmish of the Civil War was the **Battle of Valverde**, the sole Confederate victory in the New Mexico campaign, while the **Battle of Glorieta Pass** sealed the Union's dominance of the Wes t and drove the Confederate forces back into the South.

The First **Battle of Adobe Walls** was one of the largest battles fought between US Troops and the Plains Indians.

These battle accounts that exist can be very effective in uncovering the military records of your ancestor. They can tell you what regiments fought in which battles, and often include the names and ranks of many officers and enlisted men.

Battle of El Brazito: http://mexican-american.american-battlefields.com/battle/?id=14&n=Battle

Siege of Pueblo de Taos: http://worldhistoryproject.org/1847/2/3/siege-of-pueblo-de-taos

Battle of Valverde: http://www.civil-war-journeys.org/valverde_nm.htm

Battle of Glorieta Pass: http://www.civilwar.org/battlefields/glorieta-pass.html

Battle of Adobe Walls: http://montyrainey.wordpress.com/2012/06/15/the-battle-of-adobe-walls/

Common New Mexico Genealogical Issues and Resources to Overcome Them

Boundary Changes: Boundary changes are a common obstacle when researching New Mexico ancestors. You could be searching for an ancestor's record in one county when in fact it is stored in a different one due to historical county boundary changes.

The **Atlas of Historical County Boundaries** can help you to overcome that problem. It provides a chronological listing of every boundary change that has occurred in the history of New Mexico.

Atlas of Historical County Boundaries:
http://publications.newberry.org/ahcbp/documents/NM_Consolidate d_Chronology.htm#Consolidated_Chronology

Name Changes: Surname changes, variations, and misspellings can complicate genealogical research. It is important to check all spelling variations. Soundex, a program that indexes names by sound, is a useful first step, but you can't rely on it completely as some name variations result in different Soundex codes. The surnames could be different, but the first name may be different too. You can also find records filed under initials, middle names, and nicknames as well, so you will need to **get creative with surname variations** and spellings in order to cover all the possibilities. For help with surname variations read our instructional article on **How to Use Soundex**.

get creative with surname variations:
http://obituarieshelp.org/blog/?p=634

How to Use Soundex: http://obituarieshelp.org/blog/?p=505

New Mexico Genealogical Organizations and Archives

Genealogical resources include not only records, but the organizations that house them, or can direct you to them. These institutions include: *Archives, Libraries, Genealogical Societies, Family History Centers, Universities, Churches, and Museums.*

Following are links to their websites, their physical addresses, and a summary of the records you can find there.

Archives and Libraries

New Mexico Records Center and Archives – church records, census records, property records, mining records, tax records, naturalization records, military records, wills, family histories

1205 Camino Carlos Rey
Santa Fe, NM 87507
Telephone: 505-476-7948
Fax: 505-476-7909
Email: archives@state.nm.us

New Mexico Records Center and Archives:
http://www.nmcpr.state.nm.us/archives/primary.htm

National Archives Rocky Mountain Region (Denver) - Federal population censuses for all States, 1790-1930, Revolutionary War records, Pension and bounty land warrant applications, Ship's passenger lists, Indian censuses

17101 Huron Street
Broomfield, CO 80023
Telephone: 303-604-4740
Fax: 303-407-5707

National Archives Rocky Mountain Region (Denver:
http://www.archives.gov/denver/public/genealogy.html

Albuquerque Public Library - Albuquerque newspapers 1890, Territorial newspapers, Indian Census from 1885 to 1940, Dawes Rolls, Returns from U.S. Military Forts, 1800-1916, Union Soldier service records, World War I New Mexico Selective Service Draft Registration Cards, 1917-1918, U.S. Census to 1930, Catholic, Presbyterian, and Methodist Church records, City directories, Arizona vital records between 1881-1930 for many counties, Methodist Church Circuit Riding Minister Marriage Records 1870-1918 for New Mexico and Colorado, New Mexico county Death & Delayed Birth Records, Inventory of the Spanish Archives of New Mexico I, 1685-1912, Inventory of the Spanish Archives of New Mexico II, 1621-1821, Inventory of the Territorial Archives of New Mexico, 1846-1912

501 Copper Avenue, N.W.
Albuquerque, NM 87102
Telephone: 505-768-5100
Fax: 505-768-5191

Albuquerque Public Library: http://abclibrary.org/genealogy

New Mexico State Library – Civil War records, historical newspapers, historical maps, periodicals, directories, census records

1209 Camino Carlos Rey
Santa Fe, NM 87507
Telephone: 505-476-9700

New Mexico State Library: http://www.nmstatelibrary.org/

Montana Genealogical and Historical Societies

Genealogical and historical societies have access to extensive catalogues of genealogical data. They are also able to offer expert guidance for genealogical researchers. Many members are professional genealogists who are most willing to share their expertise in finding ancestors.

New Mexico Genealogical Society – huge variety of resources including church records, family histories, death indexes, burial records, census, and the New Mexico DNA Project

P.O. Box 27559
Albuquerque, NM 87125

New Mexico Genealogical Society: http://www.nmgs.org/index.php

Hispanic Genealogical Research Center of New Mexico – huge pedigree database (Great New Mexico Pedigree Database (GNMPD) and other resources for tracing Hispanic ancestors in New Mexico

Lourdes Hall, St. Pius X Campus
4060 St Joseph Pl. NW
Albuquerque, NM 87125
Telephone: 505-833-4197

Hispanic Genealogical Research Center of New Mexico: http://www.hgrc-nm.org/

Historical Society of New Mexico – wide variety of historical resources and links to every county genealogical society in New Mexico

P.O. Box 1912
Santa Fe, NM 87504

Historical Society of New Mexico: http://www.hsnm.org/

Additional New Mexico Genealogy Resources

New Mexico Mailing Lists

Mailing lists are internet based facilities that use email to distribute a single message to all who subscribe to it. When information on a particular surname, new records, or any other important genealogy information related to the mailing list topic becomes available, the subscribers are alerted to it. Joining a mailing list is an excellent way to stay up to date on New Mexico genealogy research topics. Rootsweb have an extensive listing of **New Mexico Mailing Lists** on a variety of topics.

New Mexico Mailing Lists:
http://lists.rootsweb.ancestry.com/index/usa/NM/misc.html

New Mexico Message Boards

A message board is another internet based facility where people can post questions about a specific genealogy topic and have it answered by other genealogists. If you have questions about a surname, record type, or research topic, you can post your question and other researchers and genealogists will help you with the answer. Be sure to check back regularly, as the answers are not emailed to you. The New Mexico message boards at **Rootsweb** are completely free to use.

Rootsweb:
http://boards.rootsweb.com/localities.northam.usa.states/mb.ashx

New Mexico Newspapers and Periodicals

Many genealogy periodicals and historical newspapers contain reprinted copies of family genealogies, transcripts of family Bible records, information about local records and archives, census indexes, church records, queries, land records, obituaries, court records, cemetery records, and wills. The following sites have historical New Mexico newspapers and periodicals that you can search online or on-site.

Albuquerque Public Library - Albuquerque newspapers 1890 and Territorial newspapers

501 Copper Avenue, N.W.
Albuquerque, NM 87102
Telephone: 505-768-5100
Fax: 505-768-5191

Albuquerque Public Library: http://abclibrary.org/genealogy

New Mexico State Library – historical newspapers and periodicals dating back to 1849

1209 Camino Carlos Rey
Santa Fe, NM 87507
Telephone: 505-476-9700

New Mexico State Library: http://www.nmstatelibrary.org/

GenealogyBank.com – free searchable database of New Mexico newspaper archives, 1844-1973

GenealogyBank.com:
http://www.genealogybank.com/gbnk/newspapers/explore/USA/New_Mexico/

The Online Books Page – links to historical New Mexico books and periodicals available for viewing online

The Online Books Page:
http://onlinebooks.library.upenn.edu/webbin/book/browse?type=subject&c=c&key=new+mexico

Library of Congress Digital Newspaper Directory – free searchable database of historical U.S. newspapers dating from 1690-present

Library of Congress Digital Newspaper Directory:
http://chroniclingamerica.loc.gov/search/titles/

NewspaperArchive.com – largest online database of historical newspapers in the world.

NewspaperArchive.com: http://newspaperarchive.com/

Historical New Mexico Maps and Gazetteers

Maps are an integral part of genealogical research. They help us to locate landmarks, towns, cities, parishes, states, provinces, waterways and roads and streets. They also help us to determine when and where boundary changes might have taken place, and give us a visualization of the area we're researching in.

For locating place names, a gazetteer is the best possible resource for any genealogist. Gazetteers are also sometimes called "place name dictionaries", and can help you to locate the area in which you need to conduct research. Below are links to the maps and gazetteers for research in New Mexico.

Peabody GNIS Service – New Mexico:
http://peabody.research.yale.edu/cgi-bin/Query.GNIS?ST=New%20Mexico&SU=1

Color Landform Atlas – New Mexico:
http://fermi.jhuapl.edu/states/nm_0.html

1985 U.S. Atlas: http://www.livgenmi.com/1895/NM/

New Mexico Hometown Locator:
http://newmexico.hometownlocator.com/

New Mexico City Directories

.

City directories are similar to telephone directories in that they list the residents of a particular area. The difference though is what is important to genealogists, and that is they pre-date telephone directories. You can find an ancestor's information such as their street address, place of employment, occupation, or the name of their spouse. A one-stop-shop for finding city directories in New Mexico is the **New Mexico Online Historical Directories** which contains a listing of every available online historical directory related to New Mexico..

New Mexico Online Historical Directories:
https://sites.google.com/site/onlinedirectorysite/Home/usa/nm

Albuquerque Public Library – City directories from Albuquerque, Carlsbad, Clovis, Gallup, Hobbs, Portales, Roswell, Santa Fe, and New Mexico Business Directory dating from 1903-1986

501 Copper Avenue, N.W.
Albuquerque, NM 87102
Telephone: 505-768-5100
Fax: 505-768-5191

Albuquerque Public Library: http://abclibrary.org/genealogy

New Mexico Genealogical Records

<u>Birth, Death, Marriage and Divorce Records</u> – Also known as vital records, birth, death, and marriage certificates are the most basic, yet most important records attached to your ancestor. The reason for their importance is that they not only place your ancestor in a specific place at a definite time, but potentially connect the individual to other relatives. Below is a list of repositories and websites where you can find New Mexico vital records.

In 1919, The Bureau of Vital Records and Health Statistics was created to register births and deaths that occurred in New Mexico. Copies of marriage licenses are available from the **County Clerk** of the county where the marriage license was issued. Copies of divorce decrees are available from the **District Court** where the court order was filed.

County Clerk:
http://www.sos.state.nm.us/Voter_Information/County_Clerk_Infor mation.aspx

District Court: http://www.nmcourts.gov/newface/court-interp/files/Court_State_Name_Directory_2013.pdf?updated=02082 013

Bureau of Vital Records & Health Statistics – birth and death records from 1919 to present
1105 South St. Francis Drive
Santa Fe, NM 87502
Tel: (505) 827-0121
Toll Free (866) 534-0051

Mailing Address:
New Mexico Dept. of Health
Vital Records Division
P.O Box 25767
Albuquerque, NM 87125

Bureau of Vital Records & Health Statistics:
http://www.vitalrecordsnm.org/

Albuquerque Public Library - Arizona vital records between 1881-1930 for many counties, Methodist Church Circuit Riding Minister Marriage Records 1870-1918 for New Mexico and Colorado, New Mexico county Death & Delayed Birth Records

501 Copper Avenue, N.W.
Albuquerque, NM 87102
Telephone: 505-768-5100
Fax: 505-768-5191

Albuquerque Public Library: http://abclibrary.org/genealogy

Family Search has the following indexes which can be searched online for free:

New Mexico, Births and Christenings, 1726-1918:
https://familysearch.org/search/collection/1680839

New Mexico, County Death Records, 1907-1952:
https://familysearch.org/search/collection/1966081

New Mexico, County Marriages, 1885-1954:
https://familysearch.org/search/collection/2110325

New Mexico, Deaths and Burials, 1788-1798; 1838-1955:
https://familysearch.org/search/collection/1680843

New Mexico, Deaths, 1889-1945:
https://familysearch.org/search/collection/1546466

New Mexico, Marriages, 1751-1918:
https://familysearch.org/search/collection/1680844

Census Reports

Census records are among the most important genealogical documents for placing your ancestor in a particular place at a specific time. Like BDM records, they can also lead you to other ancestors, particularly those who were living under the authority of the head of household.

Federal census records for New Mexico exist from 1850–1940 and can be found at:

New Mexico Records Center and Archives – 1850, 1860, 1870, 1880, 1885, 1900, 1910, and 1920 Federal census records

1205 Camino Carlos Rey
Santa Fe, NM 87507
Telephone: 505-476-7948
Fax: 505-476-7909
Email: archives@state.nm.us

New Mexico Records Center and Archives:
http://www.nmcpr.state.nm.us/archives/primary.htm

National Archives Rocky Mountain Region (Denver) - Federal population censuses for all States, 1790-1930, Indian censuses

17101 Huron Street
Broomfield, CO 80023
Telephone: 303-604-4740
Fax: 303-407-5707

National Archives Rocky Mountain Region (Denver):
http://www.archives.gov/denver/public/genealogy.html

National Archives – Federal census Schedules for all states, 1790-1940

8601 Adelphi Road
College Park, MD 20740-6001
Tel: 1-866-272-6272

National Archives: http://www.archives.gov/research/census/

The **Free Census Project** has transcribed many New Mexico indexes and new material is added daily

Free Census Project: http://usgwcensus.org/cenfiles/nm.htm

Access Genealogy – New Mexico county census records from 1800-1930

Access Genealogy: http://www.accessgenealogy.com/census/new-mexico-census-records.htm

African American Census Schedules Online – slave schedules, mortality schedules, slave-owners census

African American Census Schedules Online: http://www.afrigeneas.com/aacensus/

Native Americans in Census Records (US National Archives): http://www.archives.gov/research/census/native-americans/

New Mexico Church Records

Church and synagogue records are a valuable resource, especially for baptisms, marriages, and burials that took place before 1900. You will need to at least have an idea of your ancestor's religious denomination, and in most cases you will have to visit a brick and mortar establishment to view them.

Most church records are kept by the individual church, although in some denominations, records are placed in a regional archive or maintained at the diocesan level. Local Historical Societies are sometimes the repository for the state's older church records. Below are links archives that maintain church records, as well as a few databases that can be viewed online. The **Family History Library** contains many church records from a variety of denominations on microfilm.

Family History Library:
http://familysearch.org/learn/wiki/en/Family_History_Library

New Mexico Records Center and Archives – sacramental records belonging to the Archdiocese of Santa Fe and the Diocese of Gallup

1205 Camino Carlos Rey
Santa Fe, NM 87507
Telephone: 505-476-7948
Fax: 505-476-7909
Email: archives@state.nm.us

New Mexico Records Center and Archives:
http://www.nmcpr.state.nm.us/archives/primary.htm

Albuquerque Public Library – variety of Catholic, Presbyterian, and Methodist Church records
501 Copper Avenue, N.W.
Albuquerque, NM 87102
Telephone: 505-768-5100
Fax: 505-768-5191

Albuquerque Public Library: http://abclibrary.org/genealogy

Central Repositories for Denominational Records

Church of Jesus Christ of Latter-day Saints (Mormons)

Early Mormon Church records for Montana can be found on film located at the LDS Family History Library in Salt Lake City and can be searched via the **Family History Library Catalog**

Family History Library Catalog:
https://familysearch.org/eng/Library/FHLC/frameset_fhlc.asp

Baptist

American Baptist Historical Society
3001 Mercer University Dr.
Atlanta, Georgia 30341
Telephone: (678) 547-6680

American Baptist Historical Society: http://abhsarchives.org/

Presbyterian

Presbyterian Historical Society
United Presbyterian Church in the USA
425 Lombard Street
Philadelphia, Pennsylvania 19147
Telephone: (215) 627-1852

Presbyterian Historical Society: http://www.history.pcusa.org/

Roman Catholic

Archdiocese of Santa Fe
4000 St. Joseph Place N.W.
Albuquerque, NM 87120
Phone: (505) 831-8100

Archdiocese of Santa Fe: http://www.archdiocesesantafe.org/

Diocese of Gallup
711 S. Puerco Drive
Gallup, NM 87301
Phone: (505) 863-4406
Mailing Address:
P.O. Box 1338
Gallup, NM 87301

Diocese of Gallup: http://www.dioceseofgallup.org/

Diocese of Las Cruces
1280 Med Park
Las Cruces, NM 88004
Phone: (505) 523-7577
Mailing Address:
P.O. Box 16318
Las Cruces, NM 88004

Diocese of Las Cruces: http://www.dioceseoflascruces.org/

New Mexico Military Records

More than 40 million Americans have participated in some time of war service since America was colonized. The chance of finding your ancestor amongst those records is exceptionally high. Military records can even reveal individuals who never actually served, such as those who registered for the two World Wars but were never called to duty.

Below are a number of links to websites and archives that contain New Mexico military records.

New Mexico Records Center and Archives – muster rolls for the Spanish, Mexican, and Territorial periods, Adjutant General's Collection, and World War I and World War II discharges and enlistment

1205 Camino Carlos Rey
Santa Fe, NM 87507
Telephone: 505-476-7948
Fax: 505-476-7909
Email: archives@state.nm.us

New Mexico Records Center and Archives:
http://www.nmcpr.state.nm.us/archives/primary.htm

National Archives Rocky Mountain Region (Denver) -
Revolutionary War records, Pension and bounty land warrant applications

17101 Huron Street
Broomfield, CO 80023
Telephone: 303-604-4740
Fax: 303-407-5707

National Archives Rocky Mountain Region (Denver):
http://www.archives.gov/denver/public/genealogy.html

Albuquerque Public Library - Returns from U.S. Military Forts, 1800-1916, Union Soldier service records, World War I New Mexico Selective Service Draft Registration Cards, 1917-1918

501 Copper Avenue, N.W.
Albuquerque, NM 87102
Telephone: 505-768-5100
Fax: 505-768-5191

Albuquerque Public Library: http://abclibrary.org/genealogy

US Department of Veterans Affairs Nationwide Gravesite Locator – includes information on veterans and their family members buried in veterans and military cemeteries having a government grave marker.

US Department of Veterans Affairs Nationwide Gravesite Locator: http://gravelocator.cem.va.gov/

You may also find your ancestor's military records in the following databases:

United States General Index to Pension Files, 1861-1934: https://familysearch.org/search/collection/1919699

United States Index to Service Records, War with Spain, 1898: https://familysearch.org/search/collection/1919583

United States Index to Indian Wars Pension Files, 1892-1926 – military pension records of soldiers who fought in the Indian Wars between 1817 and 1898

United States Index to Indian Wars Pension Files, 1892-1926: https://familysearch.org/search/collection/1979427

United States Registers of Enlistments in the U.S. Army, 1798-1914 - index of men who enlisted in the United States Army, 1798-1914.

United States Registers of Enlistments in the U.S. Army, 1798-1914: https://familysearch.org/search/collection/1880762

United States Mexican War Pension Index, 1887-1926 - index to Mexican War pension files for service between 1846 and 1848

United States Mexican War Pension Index, 1887-1926: https://familysearch.org/search/collection/1979390

Civil War Soldiers Service Records - Service records for both Union and Confederate soldiers indexed by soldier's name, rank, and unit.

Civil War Soldier Service Records: http://go.fold3.com/civilwar_records/

New Mexico Cemetery Records

As convenient as it is to search cemetery records online, keep in mind that there are a few disadvantages over visiting a cemetery in person. They are:

1. Tombstone information is not always accurately transcribed
2. The arrangement of the graves in a cemetery can be crucial as family members are often buried next to each other or in the same grave. This arrangement is not always preserved in the alphabetical indexes that are found online.

With that information in mind, the following websites have databases that can be searched online for New Mexico Cemetery records.

New Mexico Genealogical Society – variety of church and burial records

P.O. Box 27559
Albuquerque, NM 87125

New Mexico Genealogical Society: http://www.nmgs.org/index.php

New Mexico Tombstone Transcription Project - death and burial records

New Mexico Tombstone Transcription Project:
http://www.usgwtombstones.org/newmexico/newmex.html

African American Cemeteries Online – African American, slave, and Native American cemetery records

African American Cemeteries Online:
http://africanamericancemeteries.com/

Access Genealogy – database of New Mexico cemetery record transcriptions

Access Genealogy:
http://www.accessgenealogy.com/cemetery/new-mexico-cemetery-records.htm

Find a Grave – over 100 million grave records can be searched on this site. Search can be conducted by name, location, or cemetery name.

Find a Grave: http://www.findagrave.com/

Interment.net - A free online database containing approximately 4 million cemetery records from around the world.

Interment.net: http://www.interment.net/

Billion Graves – as the name implies, you can search a billion records including headstone photos, transcriptions, cemetery records, and grave locations.

Billion Graves:
http://billiongraves.com/pages/search/index.php#cemetery

New Mexico Obituaries

Obituaries can reveal a wealth about our ancestor and other relatives. You can search our **New Mexico Newspaper Obituaries Listings** from hundreds of New Mexico newspapers online for free.

New Mexico Newspaper Obituaries Listings:
http://obituarieshelp.org/new_mexico_newspaper_obituaries.html

New Mexico Wills and Probate Records

The documents found in a probate packet may include a complete inventory of a person's estate, newspaper entries, witness testimony, a copy of a will, list of debtors and creditors, names of executors or trustees, names of heirs. They can not only tell you about the ancestor you're currently researching, but lead to other ancestors.

Probate records for the Mexican and Spanish periods are held by the **Mexican National Archives** and the **Spanish National Archives**.

Mexican National Archives: http://www.agn.gob.mx/

Spanish National Archives link to:
http://www.mcu.es/archivos/MC/AGS/

New Mexico Records Center and Archives – Miscellaneous records of wills and diaries of individuals living in New Mexico

1205 Camino Carlos Rey
Santa Fe, NM 87507
Telephone: 505-476-7948
Fax: 505-476-7909
Email: archives@state.nm.us

New Mexico Records Center and Archives:
http://www.nmcpr.state.nm.us/archives/primary.htm

National Archives Rocky Mountain Region (Denver) - Probate records from the 1850s to 1912

17101 Huron Street
Broomfield, CO 80023
Telephone: 303-604-4740
Fax: 303-407-5707

National Archives Rocky Mountain Region (Denver):
http://www.archives.gov/denver/public/genealogy.html

New Mexico Immigration and Naturalization Records

The naturalization process generated many types of records, including petitions, declarations of intention, and oaths of allegiance. These records can provide family historians with information such as a person's birth date and place of birth, immigration year, marital status, spouse information, occupation, witnesses' names and addresses, and more.

New Mexico Records Center and Archives – Declarations and Intentions, Petitions for Naturalization, Naturalization Records, Certificates of Naturalization

1205 Camino Carlos Rey
Santa Fe, NM 87507
Telephone: 505-476-7948
Fax: 505-476-7909
Email: archives@state.nm.us

New Mexico Records Center and Archives:
http://www.nmcpr.state.nm.us/archives/primary.htm

National Archives Rocky Mountain Region (Denver) - Ship's passenger lists

17101 Huron Street
Broomfield, CO 80023
Telephone: 303-604-4740
Fax: 303-407-5707

National Archives Rocky Mountain Region (Denver):
http://www.archives.gov/denver/public/genealogy.html

U.S. National Archives – Last Name Index to Naturalization Records
(New Mexico), 1860-1963

U.S. National Archives: http://www.archives.gov/denver/finding-aids/naturalization/

New Mexico Native American Records

Albuquerque Public Library - Indian Census from 1885 to 1940, Dawes Rolls

501 Copper Avenue, N.W.
Albuquerque, NM 87102
Telephone: 505-768-5100
Fax: 505-768-5191

Albuquerque Public Library: http://abclibrary.org/genealogy

Access Genealogy – New Mexico Native American census records, tribal histories, and much more

Access Genealogy: http://www.accessgenealogy.com/native/new-mexico-indian-tribes.htm

U.S. National Archives - information on American Indians who maintained their ties to Federally-recognized Tribes (1830-1970).

U.S. National Archives: http://www.archives.gov/research/native-americans/

Records of the Bureau of Indian Affairs (BIA):
http://www.archives.gov/research/guide-fed-records/groups/075.html

American Indians Records Repository - records dating from the 1700s including trust, education and other historic Indian Affairs records
American Indian Records Repository
Meritex Enterprises
17501 West 98th Street
Lenexa, KS 66219
Phone: 913-888-0601

American Indians Records Repository:
http://www.doi.gov/ost/records_mgmt/american-indian-records-repository.cfm

Missing Matriarchs – Resources for Researching Female New Mexico Ancestors

Looking for female ancestors requires an adjustment of how we view traditional records sources. A woman's identity was often under that of her husband, and often individual records for them can be difficult to locate. The following resources are effective in locating female ancestors in New Mexico where traditional records may not reveal them.

Bibliographies

1. *Women of New Mexico: Depression Era Images,* Marta Weigle (Ancient City Press, 1993)
2. *Origins of New Mexico Families,* Chavez, Fray Angelico (Museum of New Mexico Press, 1992)
3. *The Impact of Intimacy: Mexican-Anglo Inter-Marriage in New Mexico, 1821-1846,* Rebecca M. Craver (Texas Western press, 1982)
4. *Comadres: Hispanic Women of the Rio Puerco Valley,* Nasario Garcia (University of New Mexico Press, 1997)
5. *Bridges: New Mexico Black Women, 1900-1950,* Charlotte Mock (New Mexico Commission on the Study of Women, 1985)
6. *New Mexico Women: Intercultural Perspectives,* Joan M. Jenson and Doris A. Miller (University of New Mexico Press, 1986)

Selected Resources for New Mexico Women's History

Rio Grande Historical Collections
New Mexico State University
Box 3475
Las Cruces, NM 88003

Center for Southwest research
Zimmerman Library
University of New Mexico
Albuquerque, NM 87131
Tel: 505-277-9100

Common New Mexico Surnames

The following surnames are among the most common in New Mexico and are also being currently researched by other genealogists. If you find your surname here, there is a chance that some research has already been performed on your ancestor.

Aiken, Akey, Alice, Allshouse, Altman, Ambrose, Anderson, Ankeny, Ann, Armstrong, Ashbaugh, Avey, Babcock(Bokok), Bailey, Bandcen, Barnard, Bash, Beninger, Best, Blair, Blystone, Borts, Boyer, Bridget, Brown, Bruce, Bryja, Buck, Burkett, Bush, Bussard, Calhoun, Calvo, Carnahan, Carwile, Christina, Coffman, Coleman, Conrad, Cook, Coulter, Cox, Craig, Cravener, Cravner, Cribbs, Croyle, Crum, Davis, Doty, Douglas, Dunlap, Dunmire, Earhart, Eberts, Eldridge, Elizabeth, Ferner, Fiscus, Floyd, Forester, Forster, France, Frantz, Fulton, Gadsby, George, Girt, Graff, Graft, Gress, Halderman, Hall, Hankey, Hanna, Hare, Hartman, Hawk, Heart, Heasley, Heckman, Heffelfinger, Heighley, Heilman, Heinselman, Heintzelman, Helfferich, Helfrick, Henderson, Heplar, Herford, Holt, Hough, Huckuss, Huffen, Hurte, Irwin, Isman, Jackson, Jamison, Jane, Jenson, Jerald, Johns, Johnston, Jones, Jordan, Kauffman, Kennedy, Keplon, Kepple, Kerr, Kiehner, King, Kinnard, Kipple, Kirkwood, Klingensmith, Knappenberger, Lanning, Lavina, Learn, Leightley, Lewey, Lindsey, Livingston, Lockhart, Long, Macklin, Magdalina, Maltida, Mangus, Manners, Margaret, Margaretha, Married, Martin, Mawhinney, McAdvo, McCandless, McConnell, McDowell, McElfresh, McIntire, McKnight, McNutt, Means, Miller, Mohney, Moore, Morgan, Munion, Naeima, Nancy, Neueem, Newcome, Nichal, Nicholas, Niebert, Null, Ohlinger, Osenbach, Otterman, Parks, Peace, Peterman, Platt, Preilinger, Prugh, Pugh, Raeiff, Rambach, Ramsey, Rearick, Reefer, Reeg, Reigh, Remaley, Rhoades, Richards, Rising, Robbins, Rodeman, Ross, Rowe, Rupert, Rushel, Salow, Salsgiver, Savina, Schaeffer, Schall, Scheaffer, Schiecengost, Schutt, Scott, Sell, Serfoss, Shafer, Shaffer, Shannon, Sheaffer, Shearer, Shoup,

Shutt, Sikes, Silvis, Simpson, Smeltzer, Smith, Sowers, Spang, Speicher, Spence, Sprang, Sprankle, Stewart, Stitt, Stull, Taylor, Tharp, Thom, Thomas, Thompson, Townsend, Trimble, Turk, Uber, Unknown, Velma, Wagner, Waltenbaugh, Walters, Walton, Weaver, Wegely, Wehe, Weigley, Weinel, Wells, Welsh, Wigely, Willems, Williams, Wilmsin, Wilson, Woodside, Wray, Wright, Wyant, Yearyan, Yeomans, Yerian, Yockey, Young, Yount, Zerfoss

About the Author

Gary L. Morris worked from 2009 to 2014 as a professional researcher for a major player in the genealogy field. After tracing his family lineage back to 1683, he found that genealogy could be an expensive undertaking. As such, has decided to publish these helpful guides to share the valuable free information he has discovered during his career to help others trace their family lineages as inexpensively as possible. An avid genealogist himself, he hopes you will find this guide factual, thorough, helpful, and most of all, effective in helping you to find your family members.

Notes

Notes

www.ingramcontent.com/pod-product-compliance
Lightning Source LLC
Chambersburg PA
CBHW070512290526
45790CB00003B/1204